how2become

KS3 MATHS IS EASY

(NUMBERS & CALCULATIONS)

THE
REVISION
SERIES

www.How2Become.com

As part of this product you have also received FREE access to online tests that will help you to pass Key Stage 3 MATHS *(Numbers & Calculations)*.

To gain access, simply go to:

www.MyEducationalTests.co.uk

Get more products
for passing any test at:

www.How2Become.com

Orders: Please contact How2Become Ltd, Suite 14, 50 Churchill Square Business Centre, Kings Hill, Kent ME19 4YU.

You can order through Amazon.co.uk under ISBN: 9781911259268, via the website www.How2Become.com or through Gardners.com.

ISBN: 9781911259268

First published in 2017 by How2Become Ltd.

Copyright © 2017 How2Become.

Typeset for How2Become Ltd by Anton Pshinka.

Disclaimer

CONTENTS

THE
REVISION
SERIES

UNDERSTANDING THE CURRICULUM

THE NATIONAL CURRICULUM

State-funded schools are governed by a set curriculum of 'core' subjects, which must form part of a child's education. These core subjects are essential for providing key knowledge and skills, which in turn will help us to produce well-rounded and educated citizens.

In Key Stage 3 (ages 11-14), the core subjects that must be taught in schools include the following:

- **English**
- **Maths**
- **Science**
- **Art and Design**
- **Citizenship**
- **Computing**
- **Design and Technology**
- **Languages**
- **Geography**
- **History**
- **Music**
- **Physical Education**

All schools, from Key Stage 1 to Key Stage 4, must also teach Religious Studies to their students. From the age of 11, children will also be taught Sex Education. However, parents are given the option of pulling their children out from Religious Studies and Sex Education.

THE IMPORTANCE OF MATHS

The subject of maths is an integral lesson within the national curriculum. Students should be able to understand the key concepts and different mathematical formula in order to enhance their knowledge and increase their cognitive ability.

By achieving a strong level of understanding, students are able to convey their mathematical knowledge in a range of other subjects, including science, computing and geography.

The fundamental aims of the maths subject include:

- Using arithmetic to solve problems;
- Understanding the difference between accuracy and estimation;
- Expressing arithmetic using algebraic equations and formula;
- Learning how to carefully lay out sets of data using graphs and charts;
- Understanding averages in terms of mean, mode, median and range;
- Improving children's basic mathematical skills, before advancing on to more technical and challenging mathematical concepts;
- Improving children's confidence in their mathematical abilities, allowing them to grasp different topics of maths and how they can apply these techniques to their work.

In Key Stage 3, maths is broken down into several modules:

- **Numbers and Calculations;**
- **Ratio, Proportion and Rates of Change;**
- **Geometry and Measures;**
- **Working with Algebra;**
- **Probability and Statistics.**

The aforementioned modules are all used to teach students the vital skills for both academia and the outside world.

Pupils will be able to recognise different mathematical concepts and apply them to different calculations. In Key Stage 3, it is important that students are able to move fluently through the subject, and demonstrate a wide range of skills.

Key Stage 3 is a crucial time in academic terms, as it prepares students for their GCSEs. Every pupil will be required to take maths as a GCSE, and therefore having a strong knowledge in these starter years at secondary school, will put students in the position that they are expected to be in before entering their GCSEs.

MATHS SUBJECT CONTENT

Below we have broken down the aims and objectives of each 'module' for maths. This will give you some idea of what will be assessed, and how study can be improved in different areas of the mathematics subject as a whole.

NUMBERS AND CALCULATIONS

Pupils will be taught how to:

❑ Apply the concepts of the following mathematical numbers:
- *Prime numbers, factors, multiples, common factors, common multiples, highest common factor (HCF), lowest common multiple (LCM) and prime factorisation.*

❑ Use place values for working out decimals, measures and integers of any size.

❑ Order numbers in terms of positive and negative. Students should also have a strong grasp of mathematical symbols including:
- $=, \neq, \leq, \geq$

❑ Use brackets, powers, roots and reciprocals.

❑ Use different standard units of measure including:
- *Mass, length, time and money.*

❑ Round numbers up and down to the correct degree of accuracy. Students will be taught about significant figures and decimal places.

❑ Correctly use a calculator, and learn all of the key buttons on a scientific calculator.

❑ Interpret percentages as being 'a number out of 100'. Pupils will also be taught how to use percentages higher than 100%, how to convert a percentage into a fraction or decimal, and how to find the percentage of a number.

❑ Recognise square and cube numbers, and understanding the importance of powers 2, 3, 4 and 5.

❑ Interpret and compare numbers in standard form $A \times 10^N$ $1 \leq A < 10$, where N is a positive or negative integer or zero.

PROBABILITY AND STATISTICS

Pupils will be taught how to:

- ❑ Understand the probability of an outcome.
- ❑ Record, describe and analyse the frequency of outcomes of simple probability experiments involving randomness, fairness, equally and unequally likely outcomes, using mathematical language, and the use of a probability scale from 0-1.
- ❑ Enumerate data and understand information provided in the form of:
  - *Tables, grids, graphs and charts, Venn diagrams and pictograms.*
- ❑ Describe, interpret and compare information from graphical representations.
- ❑ Understand the mean, mode, median and range of a set of data, and comparing this to other similar data.
- ❑ Construct graphs and charts in order to represent a set of data. Pupils should understand what type of graph or chart works best for the data they have collated.

RATIO, PROPORTION AND RATES OF CHANGE

Pupils will be taught how to:

- ❑ Change between different standard units. For example:
  - *Length, area, time, volume and mass.*
- ❑ Use ratio notation, including reduction to simplest form.
- ❑ Use scale factors, scale diagrams and maps.
- ❑ Express one quantity as a fraction of another, where the fraction is less than 1 and greater than 1.
- ❑ Divide a given quantity into two parts in a given part:part or part:whole ratio; express the division of a quantity into two parts as a ratio.
- ❑ Understand that a multiplicative relationship between two quantities can be expressed as a ratio or a fraction.
- ❑ Relate the language of ratios and the associated calculations to the arithmetic of fractions and to linear functions.
- ❑ Solve problems involving percentage change, including:
  - *Percentage increase, percentage decrease, original value problems and simple interest in financial mathematics.*
- ❑ Solve problems involving direct and inverse proportion, including graphical and algebraic representations.
- ❑ Use compound units such as speed, unit pricing and density to solve problems.

WORKING WITH ALGEBRA

Pupils will be taught how to:

☐ Use and interpret algebraic notations, including:
- *ab in place of a x b;*
- *3y in place of y + y + y and 3 x y;*
- a^2 *in place of a x a,* a^3 *in place of a x a x a,* a^2b *in place of a x a x b;*
- $\frac{a}{b}$ *in place of a ÷ b;*
- *Coefficients written as fractions rather than as decimals;*
- *Brackets.*

☐ Substitute numerical values into formulae and expressions, including scientific formulae.

☐ Understand and use the concepts and vocabulary of expressions, equations, inequalities, terms and factors.

☐ Simplify and manipulate algebraic expressions to maintain equivalence by:
- *Collecting like terms;*
- *Multiplying a single term over a bracket;*
- *Taking out common factors;*
- *Expanding products of two or more binomials.*

☐ Recognise, sketch and produce graphs of linear and quadratic functions of one variable with appropriate scaling, using equations in x and y and the Cartesian plane.

☐ Use linear and quadratic graphs to estimate values of y for given values of x and vice versa and to find approximate solutions of simultaneous linear equations.

☐ Recognise arithmetic sequences and find the nth term.

☐ Find approximate solutions to contextual problems from given graphs of a variety of functions, including piece-wise linear, exponential and reciprocal graphs.

☐ Reduce a given linear equation in two variables to the standard form y = mx + c; calculate and interpret gradients and intercepts of graphs of such linear equations numerically, graphically and algebraically.

☐ Recognise geometric sequences and appreciate other sequences that arise.

GEOMETRY AND MEASURES

Pupils will be taught how to:

❑ Derive and apply formulae to calculate and solve problems involving:
- *Perimeter and area of triangles, parallelograms, trapezia, volume of cuboids (including cubes) and other prisms (including cylinders).*

❑ Calculate and solve problems involving: perimeters of 2-D shapes (including circles), areas of circles and composite shapes.

❑ Draw and measure line segments and angles in geometric figures, including interpreting scale drawings.

❑ Describe, sketch and draw using conventional terms and notations:
- *Points, lines, parallel lines, perpendicular lines, right angles, regular polygons, and other polygons that are reflectively and rotationally symmetric.*

❑ Use the standard conventions for labelling the sides and angles of triangle ABC, and know and use the criteria for congruence of triangles.

❑ Derive and illustrate properties of triangles, quadrilaterals, circles, and other plane figures [for example, equal lengths and angles] using appropriate language and technologies.

❑ Use Pythagoras' Theorem and trigonometric ratios in similar triangles to solve problems involving right-angled triangles.

❑ Use the properties of faces, surfaces, edges and vertices of cubes, cuboids, prisms, cylinders, pyramids, cones and spheres to solve problems in 3-D.

❑ Interpret mathematical relationships both algebraically and geometrically.

❑ Identify properties of, and describe the results of, translations, rotations and reflections applied to given figures.

❑ Identify and construct congruent triangles, and construct similar shapes by enlargement, with and without coordinate grids.

❑ Apply the properties of angles at a point, angles at a point on a straight line and vertically opposite angles.

❑ Understand and use the relationship between parallel lines and alternate and corresponding angles.

Maths is not only a core subject in schools, but is also a topic that impacts upon every aspect of our daily lives. As you can see, it is imperative that students are able to engage in mathematics, in order to improve on vital skills and knowledge.

USING THIS GUIDE

This guide focuses specifically on Key Stage 3 Maths (Numbers & Calculations). This book will cover everything you will need to know in terms of different types of numbers and basic calculations.

REMEMBER – It's really important that you have a good mathematical understanding, as this will help you through other school subjects, and in day-to-day activities.

HOW WILL I BE ASSESSED?

In Key Stage 3, children will be assessed based on Levels. These years do not count towards anything, and are simply a reflection of progression and development. The first years of secondary school are in place in order to determine whether or not pupils are meeting the minimum requirements, and are therefore an integral stage for preparing pupils for their GCSE courses.

Although these years do not count towards any final results, they do go a long way to deciphering which GCSEs you will pick up. For example, if you were excelling in Maths at KS3, you could consider taking this subject at A Level, and even Higher Education!

The subjects that you choose at GCSE will impact upon your future aspirations, including further education and career opportunities.

You will be monitored and assessed throughout these schooling years, via the following:

- Ongoing teacher assessments;
- Term progress reports;
- Summative assessments at the end of each academic year.

By the end of Key Stage 3, pupils are expected to achieve Levels 5 or 6.

THE
REVISION
SERIES

INCREASE YOUR CHANCES

Below is a list of GOLDEN NUGGETS that will help YOU and your CHILD to prepare for the Key Stage 3 maths.

Golden Nugget 1 – Revision timetables

When it comes to revising, preparation is key. That is why you need to sit down with your child and come up with an efficient and well-structured revision timetable.

It is important that you work with your child to assess their academic strengths and weaknesses, in order to carry out these revision sessions successfully.

> *TIP – Focus on their weaker areas first!*
>
> *TIP – Create a weekly revision timetable to work through different subject areas.*
>
> *TIP – Spend time revising with your child. Your child will benefit from your help and this is a great way for you to monitor their progress.*

Golden Nugget 2 – Understanding the best way your child learns

There are many different ways to revise when it comes to exams, and it all comes down to picking a way that your child will find most useful.

Below is a list of the common learning styles that you may want to try with your child:

- **Visual** – the use of pictures and images to remember information.
- **Aural** – the use of sound and music to remember information.
- **Verbal** – the use of words, in both speech and writing, to understand information.
- **Social** – working together in groups.
- **Solitary** – working and studying alone.

Popular revision techniques include: *mind mapping, flash cards, making notes, drawing flowcharts,* and *diagrams.* You could instruct your child on how to turn diagrams and pictures into words, and words into diagrams. Try as many different methods as possible, to see which style your child learns from the most.

TIP – *Work out what kind of learner your child is. What method will they benefit from the most?*

TIP – *Try a couple of different learning aids and see if you notice a change in your child's ability to understand what is being taught.*

Golden Nugget 3 – Break times

Allow your child plenty of breaks when revising. It's really important not to overwork your child.

TIP – *Practising for 10 to 15 minutes per day will improve your child's reading ability.*

TIP – *Keep in mind that a child's retention rate is usually between 30 to 50 minutes. Any longer than this, and your child will start to lose interest.*

Golden Nugget 4 – Practice, practice and more practice!

Purchase past practice papers. Practice papers are a fantastic way for you to gain understanding of how your child will be assessed.

Golden Nugget 5 – Understanding different areas in maths

As with any subject, maths has a range of different modules. Therefore, your child may find one module easier than another. We recommend that you spend time focusing on one module at a time. This will ensure that your child knows everything they should about each module – before moving on to the next.

TIP – *Know what modules you need to focus on!*

Golden Nugget 6 – Improve their confidence

Encourage your child to interact with you, their peers and their teachers. If they are struggling, they need to be able to reach out and ask for help. By asking for help, they will be able to work on their weaknesses, and therefore increase their overall performance and confidence.

TIP – Talk to your child and work through different maths questions with them.

Golden Nugget 7 – Stay positive!

The most important piece of preparation advice we can give you, is to make sure that your child is positive and relaxed about these tests.

Don't let assessments worry you, and certainly don't let them worry your child.

TIP – Make sure the home environment is as comfortable and relaxed as possible for your child.

Golden Nugget 8 – Answer the easier questions first

A good tip to teach your child is to answer all the questions they find easiest first. That way, they can swiftly work through the paper, before attempting the questions they struggle with.

TIP – Get your child to undergo a practice paper. Tell them to fill in the answers that they find the easiest first. That way, you can spend time helping your child with the questions they find more difficult.

Spend some time working through the questions they find difficult and make sure that they know how to work out the answer.

Golden Nugget 9 – Understanding mathematical terminology

The next section is a glossary containing all the mathematical terminology that your child should familiarise themselves with.

Sit down with your child and learn as many of these KEY TERMS as you can.

TIP – Why not make your child's learning fun? Write down all of the terms and cut them out individually. Do the same for the definitions.

Get your child to try and match the KEY TERM with its definition. Keep playing this game until they get them all right!

Golden Nugget 10 – Check out our other revision resources

We have a range of other KS3 Maths resources to help your child prepare for EVERY stage of their mathematical learning.

THE
REVISION
SERIES

LEARN
YOUR MATHS
TERMINOLOGY

ACUTE ANGLES	An angle less than 90°.
ALGEBRA	The part of maths where symbols and letters are used to represent numbers.
AREA	A measurement of a surface. The area of a square is base multiplied by the height.
BIDMAS	**B**rackets, **I**ndices, **D**ivision, **M**ultiplication, **A**ddition, **S**ubtraction. This shows the order you would complete a calculation with many operations.
CIRCUMFERENCE	The distance around something. It is the enclosing boundary of a curved geometric figure.
COMPOUND SHAPE	A compound shape includes two or more simple shapes.
CUBED NUMBERS	A cube number is a number multiplied by itself, three times.
DECIMAL PLACES	The position of a digit to the right of a decimal point.
DECIMAL	A type of number, for example 0.5 is equivalent to 50%.
DIAMETER	A straight line passing side-to-side through the middle of a circle.
EQUILATERAL TRIANGLE	A type of triangle. All sides and angles are of equal value. All angles are 60°.
ESTIMATING	A rough calculation or guess.
FACTOR	A factor is a number that can be divided wholly into another number. For example, 4 is a factor of 8.
FRACTIONS	A type of number, for example ½ is equivalent to a half.
FREQUENCY	The frequency of a specific data is the number of times that number occurs. (Frequent).
HIGHEST COMMON FACTOR (HCF)	To find the HCF, you need to find all of the factors of two or more numbers, and then see which number is the highest.

IMPERIAL UNITS	Imperial units of length, mass and capacity. Includes inch, foot, yard, ounce, pound, stone, pint and gallon.
ISOSCELES TRIANGLE	A type of triangle. Two sides and angles are of the same value.
LOWEST COMMON MULTIPLE (LCM)	To find the LCM, you will need to find the first few multiples of two or more numbers, and then work out the lowest number in common.
MEAN	A type of average. Add up all of the numbers and divide it by how many numbers there are.
MEDIAN	A type of average. Rearrange the numbers in ascending order. What number is in the middle?
METRIC UNITS	Metric units of length, mass and capacity. Includes mm, cm, km, mg, g, kg, ml and litres.
MODE	A type of average. What number occurs the most?
MULTIPLE	A multiple simply means 'times tables'. The multiples of 2 are 2, 4, 6, 8 and so on.
NEGATIVE NUMBER	A negative number is a number less than 0. On a scale, positive numbers move to the right, and negative numbers move to the left. Indicated by the sign '-'. For example, -4.
OBTUSE ANGLE	A type of angle. An obtuse angle is more than 90° but less than 180°.
PARALLEL LINES	Parallel lines are two or more lines that are always the same distance apart, and never touch.
PERIMETER	A measurement of a surface. The line forming the boundary of a closed geometrical figure.
PERPENDICULAR LINES	A perpendicular line is two lines which meet at a right angle (90°).
PI	The mathematic constant 3.14159... The ratio of a circle's circumference to its diameter.

POSITIVE NUMBER	A positive number is a number more than 0. On a scale, positive numbers move to the right, and negative numbers move to the left.
PROBABILITY	The extent to whether something is likely to occur.
RADIUS	The radius is a straight line from the mid-point of a circle, to the outer edge of the circle.
RANGE	A type of average. The range between the largest number and the smallest number.
RATIO	The quantitative relation between two amounts showing the number of times one value contains or is contained within the other.
REFLEX ANGLE	A type of angle. A reflex angle is more than 180° but less than 360°.
RIGHT-ANGLED TRIANGLE	A type of triangle. A triangle that has a 90° angle.
SCALENE TRIANGLE	A triangle with no equal angles or equal length sides.
SIGNIFICANT FIGURES	The digits carrying meaning. This allows us to get a rough idea. For example, 48,739. The '4' is a significant figure because it represents 40 thousand.
SIMPLIFYING FRACTIONS	A way of making a fraction easier to read by finding a whole number that can be divided equally into both the denominator and numerator. For example, 12/24 can be simplified to 1/2. Both '12' and '24' can be divided by 12.
SQUARED NUMBER	A square number is the number that is reached when multiplying two of the same numbers together. For example 9 is the square number of 3 x 3.
SYMMETRY	Symmetry is when one shape becomes exactly like another if it's flipped or rotated.
VOLUME	The amount of space that a shape or object occupies. Contained within a container.

BIDMAS AND CALCULATIONS

WHAT IS BIDMAS?

BIDMAS is an acrostic which can be used to remember how you should go about solving maths questions.

BIDMAS is a great way to remember which order you should work out operations in a calculation that has more than one operation.

The order of operations should follow BIDMAS:

Brackets   **( )**

Indices x^2

Division   **÷**

Multiplication   **X**

Addition   **+**

Subtraction   **-**

Check out our Youtube channel **CAREERVIDZ** for more information on averages.

UNDERSTAND USING EXAMPLE

EXAMPLE

Using BIDMAS, work out the following calculation:

$$8 + 4 \times 3 - 6$$

How to work it out:

- Remember the order of operations.
- In this calculation, you have addition, multiplication and subtraction.
- First, you should work out which operation needs to be worked out first. In this case, it is multiplication.
  - o $4 \times 3 = 12$
- Next, we would do the addition.
  - o $8 + 12 \ (4 \times 3) = 20$
- Finally, we would do the subtraction.
  - o $20 - 6 = 14$

ACTIVITY TIME!

Work out the following calculation:

$$100 - 3 \times (5 \times 6)$$

ACTIVITY TIME!

Work out the following calculation:

$$7 \times 4 \times 3^2 \div 2$$

Question Time!

QUESTION 1

Write what each letter of BIDMAS stands for.

B = _____

I = _____

D = _____

M = _____

A = _____

S = _____

QUESTION 2

Using BIDMAS, work out the following calculations. Try and show your working where possible.

a) 9 + 7 x 3

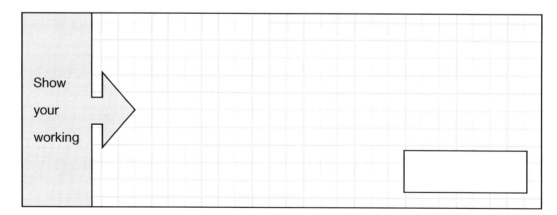

b) 22 – 4 x 5 + 1

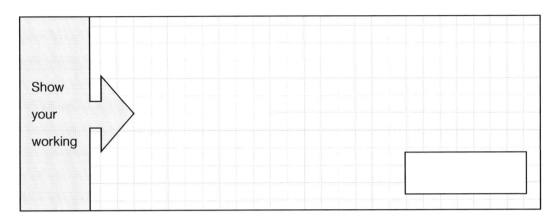

c) 5 (10 x 4) + 2

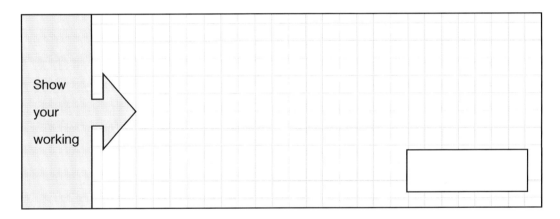

d) 9^2 + 5 x 3

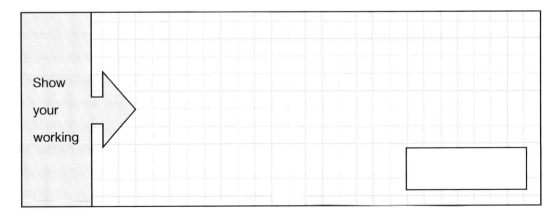

QUESTION 3

Add brackets in order to make the calculation correct.

a) $12 + 24 \div 2 = 24$

b) $4^2 + 4 \times 3 = 60$

c) $5 \times 5 + 2 \times 3 = 31$

d) $4 + 15 \div 3 \times 0 = 0$

QUESTION 4

Using BIDMAS, fill in the missing numbers. You should only use the numbers 1 to 9, and each number can only be used once.

a)

4	+		-		= 8
+		+		+	
	x	1	x		= 48
÷		x		x	
2	+		x	5	= 47
=		=		=	
8		16		33	

b)

	÷	3	×		= 24
×		×		-	
	×		-	4	= 38
×		×		+	
	-		+	2	= 2
=		=		=	
315		18		2	

c)

	+		+	7	= 12
×		×		×	
3	×		-		= 25
×		×		+	
	+		-	8	= 3
=		=		=	
15		216		22	

Answers

Q1.

B = Brackets

I = Indices

D = Division

M = Multiplication

A = Addition

S = Subtraction

Q2.

a) 30

- $7 \times 3 = 21$
- $9 + 21 = 30$

b) 1

- $4 \times 5 = 20$
- $20 + 1 = 21$
- $22 - 21 = 1$

c) 202

- $10 \times 4 = 40$
- $5 \times 40 = 200$
- $200 + 2 = 202$

d) 96

- $9 \times 9 = 81$
- $5 \times 3 = 15$
- $81 + 15 = 96$

Q3.

a)　$12 + (24 \div 2) = 24$

b)　$(4^2 + 4) \times 3 = 60$

c)　$(5 \times 5) + (2 \times 3) = 31$

d)　$4 + (15 \div 3) \times 0 = 0$　　*There are multiple possibilities for this question.

Q4

a)

4	+	7	-	3	= 8
+		+		+	
8	x	1	x	6	= 48
÷		x		x	
2	+	9	x	5	= 47
=		=		=	
8		16		33	

b)

9	÷	3	x	8	= 24
x		x		-	
7	x	6	-	4	= 38
x		x		+	
5	-	1	+	2	= 2
=		=		=	
315		18		2	

c)

1	+	4	+	7	= 12
x		x		x	
3	x	9	-	2	= 25
x		x		+	
5	+	6	-	8	= 3

| = | | = | | = | |
| 15 | | 216 | | 22 | |

THE
REVISION
SERIES

THE ORDER
OF NUMBERS

PLACE VALUES FOR WHOLE NUMBERS

When it comes to whole numbers, you can place these digits under headings. These are called PLACE VALUE HEADINGS.

Place value headings allow you to work out what each number represents. Whether its hundreds, thousands, millions and so forth.

Below I have created the place value columns which you must learn, and have presented them with an example number.

MILLIONS	HUNDRED-THOUSANDS	TEN-THOUSANDS	THOUSANDS	HUNDREDS	TENS	UNITS
4	5	8	1	2	3	6

As you can see, the above number is broken down into **columns**. These columns help you work out what each number stands for.

Let's break this number down even further!

4 000 000 = 4 million

500 000 = 5 hundred thousand

80 000 = 80 thousand

1 000 = 1 thousand

200 = 2 hundred

30 = 3 tens (thirty)

6 = 6 units

> To break down the number, begin on the right side. Moving left, put a comma after every 3 digits. This will help you to read the number.
>
> **4,581,236**

So, this number is four million, five hundred and eighty one thousand, two hundred and thirty six.

PLACE VALUES FOR DECIMALS

When it comes to decimals, you can also place these under columns. The most important thing about decimals is the DECIMAL POINT.

When working with more than one decimal, you must remember to line up the decimal points to be able to compare them correctly.

Below I have created the place value columns which you must learn, and have presented them with an example number.

HUNDREDS	TENS	UNITS	DECIMAL POINT	TENTHS	HUNDREDTHS	THOUSANDTHS
2	8	7	.	1	3	5

As you can see, the above number is broken down into **columns**. These columns help you work out what each number stands for.

<u>Let's break this number down even further!</u>

200.000 = 2 hundred

80.000 = 8 tens (eighty)

7.000 = 7 units

0.100 = 1 tenth

0.030 = 3 hundredths

0.005 = 5 thousandths

> Remember to always line up the decimal points!
>
> This is particularly important when you are working with multiple decimals.

So this number would read as two hundred and eighty seven POINT one three five.

HOW TO PUT NUMBERS IN ORDER

It is pretty simple to order numbers from smallest to biggest, but just to refresh your memory, I am going to teach you a couple of tricks.

| 85 | 9 | 12 | 723 | 3 | 962 |

To rearrange these numbers from smallest to biggest:

STEP 1

Create three groups, one for the numbers with only 1 digit, one for the numbers with 2 digits and one for the numbers with 3 digits.

1 digits	2 digits	3 digits
9 3	85 12	723 962

STEP 2

Rearrange these in their groups (from smallest to biggest).

1 digits	2 digits	3 digits
3 9	12 85	723 962

STEP 3

So, in ascending order, from smallest to biggest, the numbers are:

3 9 12 85 723 962

HOW TO PUT NUMBERS IN ORDER

To rearrange decimals from smallest to biggest is a little bit trickier. As long as you pay close attention to the numbers and the decimal point, you should be fine!

| 0.01 | 0.1 | 0.52 | 2.3 | 0.0023 | 3.01 |

To rearrange these numbers from smallest to biggest:

STEP 1

The best thing to do is line these numbers up using the decimal point.

0.01

0.1

2.52

2.3

0.0023

3.01

> You need to focus on the numbers in relation to the decimal point.
>
> In the tenths column, you know that '3' is smaller than '5', so this number would be smaller (assuming the number before the decimal point was the same).

STEP 2

So, in ascending order, from smallest to biggest, the numbers are:

0.0023   0.01   0.1   2.3   2.52   3.01

MATHEMATICAL SYMBOLS

Most people know the symbols for addition, subtraction, multiplication and division, however, there are a few more symbols that you should be aware of.

< less than	**≤** less than or equal to
> more than	**≥** more than or equal to
= equal to	**≠** not equal to

$3 < 6$	$12 > 7$	$4 + 4 = 6 + 2$
(3 is less than 6)	(12 is more than 7)	(8 is equal to 8)
$3 + 5 \neq 6 + 1$	$1 \leq 5$	$5 \geq 4$
(8 is not equal to 7)	(1 is less than or equal to 5)	(5 is more than or equal to 4)

ACTIVITY TIME!

Try and have a go at using each of the above symbols. A good way to remember the difference between < and > is that the wide open side points to the larger number, and the small closed side points to the smaller number!

$$< \quad > \quad = \quad \neq \quad \leq \quad \geq$$

Question Time!

QUESTION 1

Write the value of the underlined number.

a) 3_6_8

b) _4_837

c) 85.7_2_

d) 0._8_953

QUESTION 2

Write the following numbers in words.

a) 943

b) 43,301

c) 9,048,410

_____

_____

QUESTION 3

Write the following in numbers.

a) One hundred thousand, three hundred and twenty seven

```



```

b) One hundred and seven million, eight hundred and twenty one thousand, four hundred and six

```



```

c) Two hundred and sixty three thousand, one hundred and ninety seven, point one

```



```

QUESTION 4

Write the following numbers in ascending order.

a) 9825   63   168   653.5   42.6   0.6   0.0036

_____ _____ _____ _____ _____ _____ _____

b) 4985   698   49.65   45.036   468.4   63   401.01

_____ _____ _____ _____ _____ _____ _____

c) 36.3025   3.3236   3.0025   360.36   36.3   36.321   3.0354

_____ _____ _____ _____ _____ _____ _____

QUESTION 5

Write < or > between the following numbers.

a) 98 ☐ 468

b) 6.3 ☐ 4.2

c) 345 ☐ 34.5

d) 69.65 ☐ 69.96

QUESTION 6

Write = or ≠ between the following numbers.

a) £5.20 ☐ 520p

b) 4km ☐ 4000m

c) 100cm ☐ 10m

d) 1000l ☐ 1ml

Answers

Q1.

a) Tens

b) Thousands

c) Hundredths

d) Tenths

Q2.

a) Nine hundred and forty three

b) Forty three thousand, three hundred and one

c) Nine million, forty eight thousand, four hundred and ten

Q3.

a) 100,327

b) 107,821,406

c) 263,197.1

Q4.

a) 0.0036   0.6   42.6   63   168   653.5   9825

b) 45.036   49.65   63   401.01   468.4   698   4985

c) 3.0025   3.0354   3.3236   36.3   36.3025   36.321   360.36

Q5.

a) 98 < 468

b) 6.3 > 4.2

c) 345 > 34.5

d) 69.65 < 69.96

Q6.

a) £5.20 = 520p

b) 4km = 4000m

c) 100cm ≠ 10m

d) 1000l ≠ 1ml

POSITIVE AND NEGATIVE NUMBERS

POSITIVE AND NEGATIVE NUMBERS

When working out how to order numbers, it is important that you know the difference between POSITIVE and NEGATIVE numbers!

Positive Numbers ⟹ any number ABOVE '0'.

Negative Numbers ⟹ any number BELOW '0'.

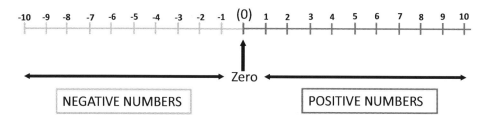

NEGATIVE NUMBERS   POSITIVE NUMBERS

Negative numbers are another word for 'minus'.

Negative numbers are often used to refer to really cold temperatures. The higher the number, the colder it is.

Positive numbers are another word for 'plus'.

Positive numbers are often used to refer to warm temperatures. The higher the number, the hotter it is.

NOTE: a lot of people make the mistake that -10 is higher than -7 because the number is bigger – these people would be wrong! -10 is further down the number line which means the number is further away from zero, and is therefore smaller.

ADDING AND SUBTRACTING NEGATIVE NUMBERS

If you are adding negative numbers ⟹ count towards the **right**.

If you are subtracting negative numbers ⟸ count towards the **left**.

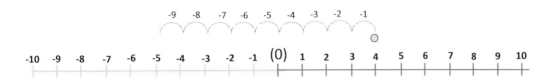

What is 4 – 9?

Step 1 = find '4' on the number line. Remember if there is no sign before a number, it is positive (+).

Step 2 = you are subtracting, which means you need to count backwards i.e. to the left.

Step 3 = after counting back 9, you should end up on -5. This is the answer.

There are a few rules you need to be aware of when it comes to signs.

If two signs appear next to each other in a sum you are doing, like 2+-2 (2 plus -2), you need to know what to do.

If you are multiplying or dividing, you will also need to know what sign to use.

COMBINING SIGNS IN SUMS

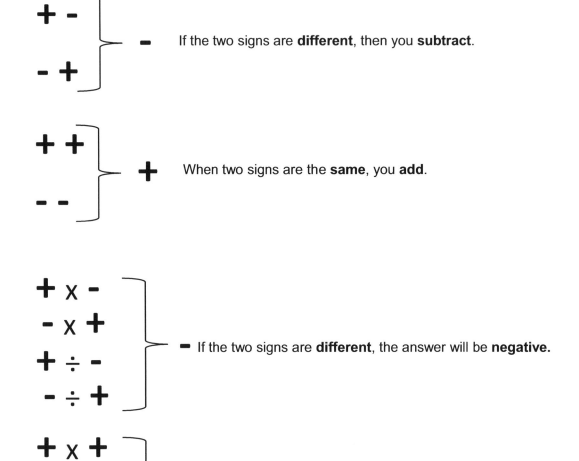

+ -
- + — If the two signs are **different**, then you **subtract**.

+ +
- - **+** When two signs are the **same**, you **add**.

+ × -
- × +
+ ÷ -
- ÷ + **—** If the two signs are **different**, the answer will be **negative**.

+ × +
- × -
+ ÷ +
- ÷ - **+** If the two signs are the **same**, the answer will be **positive**.

Question Time!

QUESTION 1

Using the number line to help:

a) What is 9 + -4?

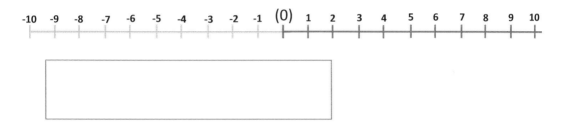

b) What is 6 - -3?

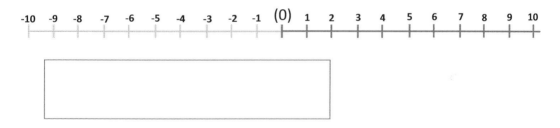

c) What is -9 ÷ 3?

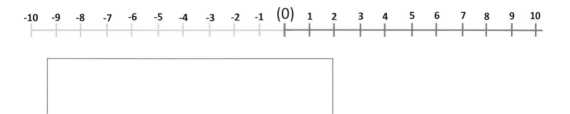

QUESTION 2

Arrange these numbers from coldest to hottest.

$$15°C \quad -12°C \quad 35°C \quad -11°C \quad 0°C \quad 1°C \quad -3°C$$

QUESTION 3

Study the graph below and answer the following questions.

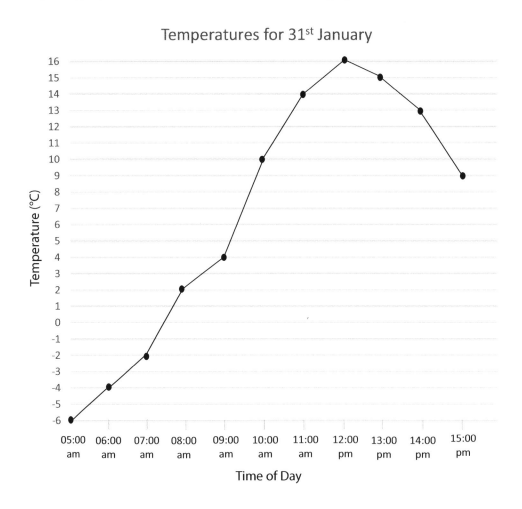

Temperatures for 31st January

a) What was the temperature at 06:00 am?

b) Based on the times recorded, how many occasions on the 31st January was the temperature **BELOW** freezing?

c) What was the difference in temperature between 05:00am and 11:00am?

Answers

Q1.

a) 5

  • + and – equals a minus

b) 9

  • – and – equals a plus

c) -3

  • 9 ÷ 3 = 3

  • - ÷ + the answer will be negative.

Q2.

-12°C   -11°C   -3°C   0°C   1°C   15°C   35°C

Q3.

a) -4°C

b) 3

c) 20°C

THE REVISION SERIES

ROUNDING AND ESTIMATING

ROUNDING UP OR ROUNDING DOWN

It is important that you know how to correctly round numbers up and down.

When the units are **LESS THAN 5**, you will round down.

When the units are **MORE THAN**, you will round up.

If the unit **IS** 5, you will also round up!

There are different ways you could be asked to round a number up or down. This is usually asked by using the words 'to the nearest'.

To the nearest **ten** (10)	To the nearest **hundred** (100)	To the nearest **thousand** (1,000)
To the nearest **ten thousand** (10,000)	To the nearest **hundred thousand** (100,000)	To the nearest **million** (1,000,000)
	To the nearest **whole number**	

EXAMPLE 1

Round **213** to the nearest ten.

Step 1 = look at the last digit = '3'.

Step 2 = work out whether the last digit is between 1 and 4, or 5 and 9.

Step 3 = you should know to round the number down because '3' is between 1 and 4.

Step 4 = so, 213 to the nearest ten = 210.

EXAMPLE 2

Round **3,982** to the nearest hundred.

Step 1 = look at the tens digit = '8'.

Step 2 = work out whether the last digit is between 1 and 4, or 5 and 9.

Step 3 = you should know to round the number up because '8' is between 5 and 9.

Step 4 = so, 3,982 to the nearest hundred = 4,000.

NOTE: because you rounded the 8 up, the number will change to 4,000. (982 is close to 1,000).

EXAMPLE 3

Round **3,449** to the nearest thousand.

Step 1 = look at the hundreds digit = '4'.

Step 2 = work out whether the last digit is between 1 and 4, or 5 and 9.

Step 3 = you should know to round the number down because '4' is between 1 and 4.

Step 4 = so, 3,449 to the nearest thousand = 3,000

ROUNDING UP OR ROUNDING DOWN

Sometimes, you will be asked to round a number to a given number of decimal places (d.p.)

The KEY thing to remember when rounding up a number to so many decimal places, is to look at the next number after the decimal place.

How to round a number to a decimal place:

STEP 1

Identify the number of decimal places you are trying to work out. For example, for 2 d.p. you will need to look at the second number AFTER the decimal point.

STEP 2

Then, look at the next digit to the right of this number. This is called the **DECIDER**.

- If it's 5 or higher, you will round up.

- If it's 4 or less, you will leave the number as it is.

EXAMPLE

Work out what 69.659 is to 2 d.p.

Step 1 = Identify the number of decimal places (2). So, the second number after the decimal point is 5.

Step 2 = Next, identify the decider (the next number) which is 9. Because '9' is higher than 5, this means we must round up!

Step 3 = So, to 2 d.p. this number would be 69.66

ROUNDING TO SIGNFICANT FIGURES (S.F.)

Sometimes, you will be asked to round a number to a significant figure. This is very similar to rounding to decimal places, except that you will focus on the number.

How to round a number to significant figures:

STEP 1

Identify the number of significant figures you are working with. For example, if you are trying to work out 2 s.f. then you will focus on the **SECOND** digit.

STEP 2

Then, look at the next digit to the right of this number. This is called the **DECIDER**.

• If it's 5 or higher, you will round up.

• If it's 4 or less, you will leave the number as it is.

STEP 3

Once you have rounded the number, you should fill up the gaps to complete the number (zeroes will be needed up to the decimal point).

EXAMPLE

Work out 2368.5 to 3 s.f.

Step 1 = identify the number of significant figures (3). So, the third number is (6).

Step 2 = next, identify the decider (the next number) which is 8. Because '8' is higher than 5, this means we must round up!

Step 3 = So, to 3 s.f. the number would be 2370

ESTIMATING AND GUESSWORK

Sometimes, you won't be asked to work out the ACTUAL answer, and instead might be asked to ESTIMATE the answer.

This is the only time when accuracy is not so important!

To estimate:

STEP 1

Round everything off. This is your chance to simplify the calculation. For example, you may wish to round everything off to 1 s.f.

STEP 2

Next, you can do the calculation. Be sure to show all of your working out. This way, the examiner is able to see your thought process.

EXAMPLE

Estimate the value of $\dfrac{78.8 \times 12}{18}$

STEP 1

Round all the numbers off $= \dfrac{80 \times 10}{20}$

STEP 2

Work out the calculation $= 80 \times 10 \approx 800$ $800 \div 20 = 40$

KNOW THE SYMBOL!

$\approx$ means 'almost equal to'.

Question Time!

QUESTION 1

Round:

a) 3658 to 1 s.f.

b) 0.3657 to 1 d.p.

c) 0.00768 to 3 s.f.

d) 659.4756 to 3 d.p.

e) 1658.9 to 2 s.f.

f) 0.32564 to 3 d.p.

QUESTION 2

Give:

a) 16.0368 to the nearest whole number.

b) 20,236 to the nearest ten.

c) 369,168 to the nearest hundred thousand.

d) 6,096,254 to the nearest million.

e) 8,369,255 to the nearest ten.

f) 31.569 to the nearest whole number.

QUESTION 3

Estimate the value of the following:

a) $\dfrac{96.2 \times 6.8}{5}$

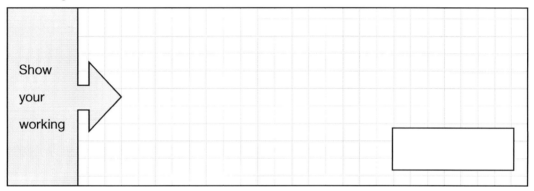

b) $4.8^2 \times 3067$

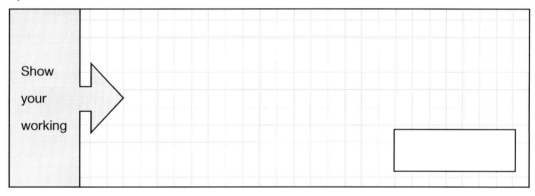

c) $(3.6 \times 32) \times 62.1$

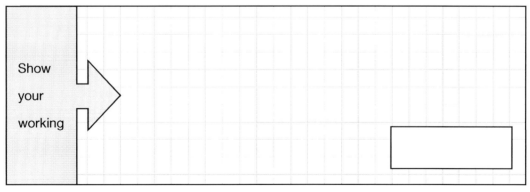

d) 9875 ÷ 47

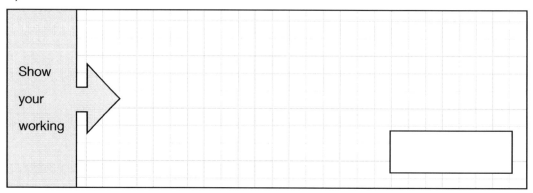

e) 168.5 x 357

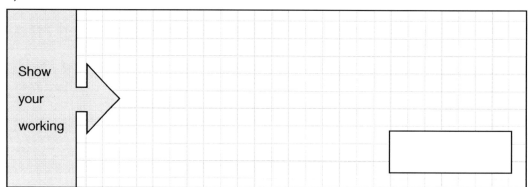

f) $\dfrac{98.4 \times 13}{22.2}$

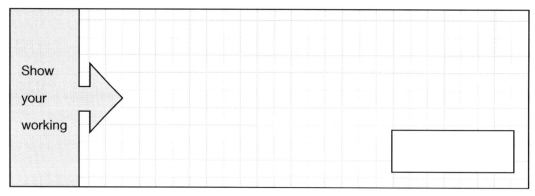

Answers

Q1.

a) 4000

b) 0.4

c) 0.01

d) 659.476

e) 1700

f) 0.326

Q2.

a) 16

b) 20,240

c) 400,000

d) 6,000,000

e) 8,369,260

f) 32

Q3.

a) 200
- 100 x 10 = 1,000
- 1,000 ÷ 5 = 200

b) 75,000
- 5 x 5 = 25
- 25 x 3000 = 75,000

c) 7,200
- 4 x 30 = 120
- 120 x 60 = 7,200

d) 200
- 10,000 ÷ 50 = 200

e) 80,000
- 200 x 400 = 80,000

f) 50
- 100 x 10 = 1,000
- 1,000 ÷ 20 = 50

HOW ARE YOU GETTING ON?

ADDING AND SUBTRACTING

HOW TO ADD ANY NUMBER

The key thing to remember when it comes to adding is to line up the numbers.

Let's use an example to help you understand:

Work out 438 + 29

h t u

438
+ 29

Step 1 = line the numbers up starting from the right column.

h t u

438
29
_____
7
1

Step 2 = add the units column (8 + 9 = 17). The '1' needs to be carried over to the tens column.

h t u

438
29
_____
6 7
1

Step 3 = add the tens column (3 + 2 = 5). Remember to add the '1' that we carried over. (3 + 2 + 1 = 6).

h t u

438
29
_____
4 6 7
1

Step 4 = there is no number to add the 4 to, so it would just be '4'.

Remember to carry over any numbers!

Remember your place value headings! See the chapter on this on pages 37 to 39.

HOW TO SUBTRACT ANY NUMBER

The key thing to remember when it comes to subtracting, is to line up the numbers.

Let's use an example to help you understand:

Work out 438 - 29

```
   h t u
   4 3 8
 -   2 9
```
Step 1 = line the numbers up starting from the right column.

```
   h t u
    2  1
   4 3 8
     2 9
         9
```
Step 2 = subtract the units column. You can't subtract 8 by 9, so you have to borrow from the next column. (The 3 becomes a 2, because we borrowed 1. Put that '1' by the 8 which makes the number 18) So 18 – 9 = 9

```
   h t u
    2  1
   4 3 8
     2 9
     0 9
     1
```
Step 3 = subtract the tens column (2 - 2 = 0).

```
   h t u
    2  1
   4 3 8
     2 9
   4 0 9
```
Step 4 = there is no number to subtract the 4 from, so it would just be '4'.

You may have to borrow from the next column! Remember to carry over any numbers!

Remember your place value headings!

THINGS TO REMEMBER FOR ADDING AND SUBTRACTING

I have outlined a few things that you should be aware of when adding or subtracting:

- Make sure that the digits are written in the correct columns. Remember your **PLACE VALUE HEADINGS.**

- Always write the numbers so that all of the numbers finish in the **UNITS** column.

- If numbers need to be carried over, remember to include these when adding up the column.

- If you are subtracting a large number from a small number, you will need to **BORROW** from the column to the left. Remember to cancel down the number you've borrowed from (i.e. 7 will become 6). That means you've borrowed '1' which can be used with the small number to be able to subtract the large number.

- If you have borrowed from a column, once the number is placed in the column you are working out, remember to read the number correctly. (So, if you borrowed 1 and put it with the number 4, you would have '14'.

Question Time!

QUESTION 1

Circle **three** of the five numbers which **add** up to **345**.

| 38 | 124 | 158 | 133 | 183 |

QUESTION 2

Below are five digit cards. Using each card **once**, complete the sum in order for the answer to be correct.

| 1 | 2 | 3 | 4 | 5 |

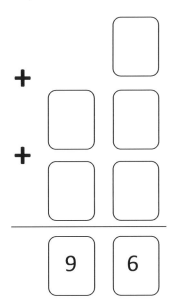

QUESTION 3

Work out the following calculations:

a)
```
  1294
+  732
_____

_____
```

b)
```
  2195
+  243
_____

_____
```

c)
```
  24697
-  1564
_____

_____
```

d)
```
   972
-  678
_____

_____
```

QUESTION 4

Fill in the missing numbers in order to make the calculation correct.

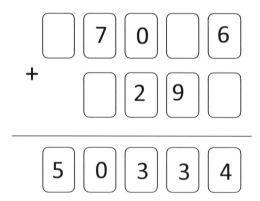

QUESTION 5

Fill in the missing numbers in order to make the calculation correct.

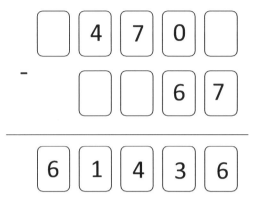

QUESTION 6

Below we have a grid containing letters from A to E.

The total for each column and row is shown

A	A	A	B	D	24
A	A	B	B	D	20
A	B	B	C	E	21
A	B	C	C	E	22
A	B	C	D	E	23
30	18	16	14	32	

Work out what each letter stands for.

A =

B =

C =

D =

E =

Answers

Q1.

38   124   183

Q2.

```
        1
  +
     4     2
  +
     5     3
  _____
     9     6
```

There are several possible answers.

Q3.

a) 2,026

b) 2,438

c) 23,133

d) 294

Q4.

```
    4  7  0  3  6
  +
          3  2  9  8
  _____
    5  0  3  3  4
```

Q5.

$$6 \quad 4 \quad 7 \quad 0 \quad 3$$
$$- \qquad 3 \quad 2 \quad 6 \quad 7$$
$$\overline{6 \quad 1 \quad 4 \quad 3 \quad 6}$$

Q6.

A = 6

B = 2

C = 3

D = 4

E = 8

MULTIPLYING AND DIVIDING

HOW TO MULTIPLY ANY NUMBER

Multiplications are quite tricky if you have no idea what you are doing. Here, we're going to teach you two methods!

1	2	3	4	5	6	7	8	9	10
2	4	6	8	10	12	14	16	18	20
3	6	9	12	15	18	21	24	27	30
4	8	12	16	20	24	28	32	36	40
5	10	15	20	25	30	35	40	45	50
6	12	18	24	30	36	42	48	54	60
7	14	21	28	35	42	49	56	63	70
8	16	24	32	40	48	56	64	72	80
9	18	27	36	45	54	63	72	81	90
10	20	30	40	50	60	70	80	90	100

A good place to start is to make sure that you have a solid grip on your times tables.

THE GRID METHOD

Let's use an example to help you understand:

Work out 456 x 17

Step 1 = 400 (hundreds)
50 (tens)
6 (units)

Step 2 = 10 (tens)
7 (units)

X	400	50	6
10			
7			

Step 3 = multiply all of the columns by the rows.

X	400	50	6
10	4,000	500	60
7	2,800	350	42

Step 4 = working along each row, add up the totals.

X	400	50	6	Totals
10	4,000	500	60	4,560
7	2,800	350	42	3,192

Step 5 = 4,560 + 3,192 = **7,752**

THE VERTICAL METHOD

Let's use an example to help you understand:

Work out 214 x 44

Step 1 = begin by lining up the numbers in the correct columns.
Step 2 = multiply the top numbers by the unit (4) in the bottom number.

```
        h   t   u
        2   1   4
            4   4
        _____
        8   5   6
            1
```

Step 3 = after you have multiplied the top numbers by the unit in the bottom number, multiply the top number by the number of tens in the bottom number (40).

(40 x 4)   *(40 x 10)*   *(40 x 200)*

```
  h   t   u           h   t   u           h   t   u
  2   1   4           2   1   4           2   1   4
      4   4               4   4               4   4
  _____         _____         _____
  8   5   6           8   5   6           8   5   6
      1                   1                   1
  1   6   0           1   6   0           1   6   0
  _____
                      4   0   0           4   0   0
                      _____
                                          8   0   0   0
                                          _____
```

Step 4 = add up all of the rows = 856 + 160 + 400 + 8,000 = **9,416**

HOW TO DIVIDE ANY NUMBER

Most people hate dividing! However, we're going to break down two methods to help you divide any number.

THE SHORT DIVISION METHOD

Let's use an example to help you understand:

Work out $504 \div 9$

$$9\overline{)504}$$

Step 1 = begin by laying out the question as shown:

$$9\overline{)5^50\,4}$$

Step 2 = how many times does 9 go into 5 = 0. Because the 5 doesn't go into 9, you need to move the 5 just above the 0 to make (50).

$$9\overline{)\,^5\,5^50\,4}\quad\overset{5}{}$$

Step 3 = how many times does 9 go into 50 = 5 (put this on top of the line above the (50). It has a remainder of 5 (put this next to the 4 to make (54)).

$$9\overline{)\,^5\,5^50\,4}\quad\overset{56}{}$$

Step 4 = how many times does 9 into 54 = 6. Put the 6 on top of the line next to the 5.

Step 5 = so the correct answer is 56.

Sometimes you will be left with a remainder! If you can't divide any more you will just write the number with 'remainder (r)...'

THE LONG DIVISION METHOD

Let's use an example to help you understand:

Work out 2,640 ÷ 20

$$20 \overline{) 2\ 6\ 4\ 0}$$

Step 1 = how many times does 20 go into 2 = 0.

$$20 \overline{) 2\ 6\ 4\ 0}$$
0 1

Step 2 = how many times does 20 go into 26 = 1 (Remainder of 6). Underneath the 26, write the whole number that goes into 26 (20). Subtract this from the 26 to find the remainder (6).

$$20 \overline{) 2\ 6\ 4\ 0}$$
0 1
2 0 ↓
6 4

Step 3 = now you are working with 64. How many times does 20 go into 64 = 3 (Remainder of 4). Underneath the 64, write the whole number that goes into 64 (60) and subtract that by the 64.

0 1 3
$$20 \overline{) 2\ 6\ 4\ 0}$$
2 0 ↓
6 4
− 6 0
4

Step 4 = Now you are working with 40. How many times does 20 go into 40 = 2. Underneath the 40, write the whole number that goes into 40 (40), and subtract the two numbers. This gives you 0, which means the sum is complete.

Step 5 = 2,640 ÷ 20 = **132**

0 1 3 2
$$20 \overline{) 2\ 6\ 4\ 0}$$
2 0 ↓
6 4
− 6 0
4 0
4 0
0 0

Question Time!

QUESTION 1

a) Here is a number machine.

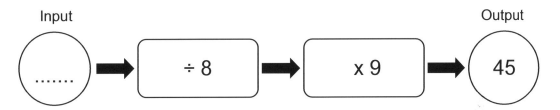

Work out the input when the output of the machine is 45.

b) Here is the same machine again.

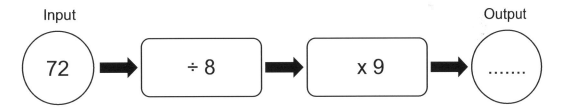

Work out the output when the input of the machine is 72.

QUESTION 2

Work out the following calculation using the multiplication grid below.

658 x 67

X	600	50	8
60			
7			

QUESTION 3

Work out the following calculations:

a)

```
  1 2 3 4
X        6
_____

_____
```

b)

```
    5 3 6
X       8
_____

_____
```

c)

```
    _____
7 ) 9 4 9 9
```

d)

```
    _____
3 ) 9 5 9 7
```

QUESTION 4

Using the long division method, work out the following calculation:

4352 ÷ 32

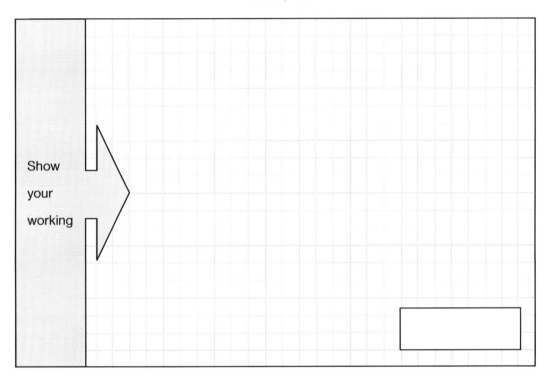

Show your working

QUESTION 5

Complete the following sums by writing in the correct sign: **+ - x** or **÷**.

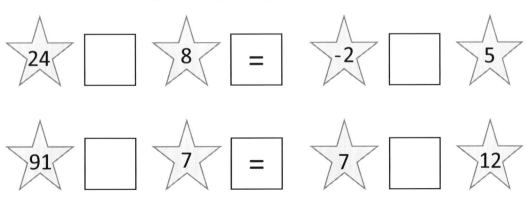

QUESTION 6

Complete the multiplication grid below.

X	3	☐	☐	7
4	12	20	☐	28
☐	33	☐	99	77
5	15	25	☐	35
☐	21	☐	63	49

Answers

Q1.

a) 40

- $45 \div 9 = 5$
- $5 \times 8 = 40$
- So, $40 \div 8 = 5$ $5 \times 9 = 45$

b) 81

- $72 \div 8 = 9$ $9 \times 9 = 81$

Q2.

44,086

X	600	50	8
60	36,000	3,000	480
7	4,200	350	56

- $36,000 + 3,000 + 480 = 39,480$
- $4,200 + 350 + 56 = 4,606$
- $39,480 + 4,606 = 44,086$

Q3.

a) 7,404

b) 4,288

c) 1,357

d) 3,199

Q4.

```
        0 1 3 6
3 2 │ 4 3 5 2
        3 2
       ─────
        1 1 5
          9 6
         ─────
          1 9 2
          1 9 2
         ─────
          0 0 0
```

Q5.

$24 \div 8 = -2 + 5$

$91 - 7 = 7 \times 12$

Q6.

X	3	5	9	7
4	12	20	36	28
11	33	55	99	77
5	15	25	45	35
7	21	35	63	49

HOW ARE YOU GETTING ON?

MULTIPLES, FACTORS AND PRIMES

MULTIPLES

Multiples are just another word for 'TIMES TABLES'.

X	1	2	3	4	5	6	7	8	9	10
1	1	2	3	4	5	6	7	8	9	10
2	2	4	6	8	10	12	14	16	18	20
3	3	6	9	12	15	18	21	24	27	30
4	4	8	12	16	20	24	28	32	36	40
5	5	10	15	20	25	30	35	40	45	50
6	6	12	18	24	30	36	42	48	54	60
7	7	14	21	28	35	42	49	56	63	70
8	8	16	24	32	40	48	56	64	72	80
9	9	18	27	36	45	54	63	72	81	90
10	10	20	30	40	50	60	70	80	90	100

TRY TO LEARN AS MANY TIMES TABLES OFF BY HEART!

MULTIPLES

How to find the least common multiple (lcm):

Finding the 'common' multiples of numbers means finding a number that they both have in common.

EXAMPLE

Find the lowest common multiple of 2 and 5.

Step 1

Write out the first few multiples of 2.

2, 4, 6, 8, 10...

Step 2

Write out the first few multiples of 5.

5, 10, 15, 20, 25...

Step 3

Find the lowest multiple that both 2 and 5 have in common.

Step 4

The lowest common multiple for 2 and 5 is 10. (There is no smaller number that is a multiple of 2 and 5, therefore this is the correct answer).

ACTIVITY TIME!

Find the lowest common multiple of the following:

- 6 and 8
- 12 and 15

FACTORS

Factors are numbers that can be divided EXACTLY into other numbers.

EXAMPLE

Work out the factors of 60.

Step 1

What numbers can be divided into 60?

- $1 \times 60 = 60$
- $2 \times 30 = 60$
- $3 \times 20 = 60$
- $4 \times 15 = 60$
- $5 \times 12 = 60$
- $6 \times 10 = 60$

Step 2

Write out the numbers in ascending order.

So, the factors of 60 are:

1   2   3   4   5   6   10   12   15   20   30   60

ACTIVITY TIME!

Work out the factors for the following numbers:

- 84
- 105

FACTORS

How to find the highest common factor (hcf):

Finding the 'common' factor of two or more numbers means finding a number that factorises into each of those numbers.

EXAMPLE

Find the highest common factor of 12 and 30.

Step 1

Work out the factors of 12.

- 1, 2, 3, 4, 6, 12

Step 2

Work out the factors of 30.

- 1, 2, 3, 5, 6, 10 15, 30

Step 3

Look out for the common factors. What numbers occur in both sets?

- 1, 2, 3, 6

Step 4

So the highest common factor is 6.

ACTIVITY TIME!

Find the highest common factor of the following:

- 24 and 36
- 90 and 175

PRIME FACTORS

EVERY number can be written as a PRODUCT of prime numbers.

PRODUCT = MULTIPLY or TIMES

THE FACTOR TREE

The best way to work out the prime factors of a number is via a factor tree.

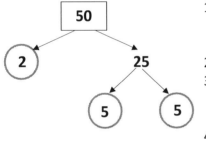

1) Find two factors to split the number (you can split the number any way you would like – you'll still end up with the same result.
2) Every time you find a prime number, circle it!
3) Keep going until you can no longer find any factors (when you're left with all prime numbers).
4) The numbers you have circled are your prime factors!

The prime factors of 50:
2 x 5 x 5

PRIME NUMBERS

Prime numbers are numbers that cannot be divided by anything else apart from the number 1 and itself. All prime numbers up to 100 have been shaded in the grid below.

1	2	3	4	5	6	7	8	9	10
11	12	13	14	15	16	17	18	19	20
21	22	23	24	25	26	27	28	29	30
31	32	33	34	35	36	37	38	39	40
41	42	43	44	45	46	47	48	49	50
51	52	53	54	55	56	57	58	59	60
61	62	63	64	65	66	67	68	69	70
71	72	73	74	75	76	77	78	79	80
81	82	83	84	85	86	87	88	89	90
91	92	93	94	95	96	97	98	99	100

Always remember:

1) The number 1 is NOT a prime number.

2) The number 2 is the ONLY even prime number.

3) Apart from the numbers 2 and 5, all prime numbers end in 1, 3, 7 or 9.

4) Relating back to my previous point, NOT ALL numbers ending in 1, 3, 7 or 9 will be prime.

HOW TO WORK OUT PRIME NUMBERS

To work out whether a number is a prime number, there are a couple of things that you can do.

1) If the number is even (2 being the exception) then you can automatically rule this out. This will not be a prime number.

2) If the number does not end in 1, 3, 7 or 9, you can automatically get rid of it. This will not be a prime number.

3) Try dividing by the numbers 3 or 7. If it does divide by either of these numbers, then it is not prime. If it doesn't divide by these numbers, then it is prime. NOTE, this only works for prime numbers up to 120!

ACTIVITY TIME!

Work out whether the following numbers are prime numbers:

- 52

- 59

- 61

- 191

Question Time!

QUESTION 1

Circle ALL of the prime numbers.

17   45   49   12   64   91   50   4   5   18   30   15

QUESTION 2

Circle ALL the numbers which are a factor of 90.

17   45   49   12   64   91   50   4   5   18   30   15

QUESTION 3

Find the **lowest common multiple** of 8 and 12.

Show your working

QUESTION 4

Is the number prime? Circle yes or no.

163   **YES / NO**

57   **YES / NO**

149   **YES / NO**

QUESTION 5

Find the **highest common factor** of 72 and 48.

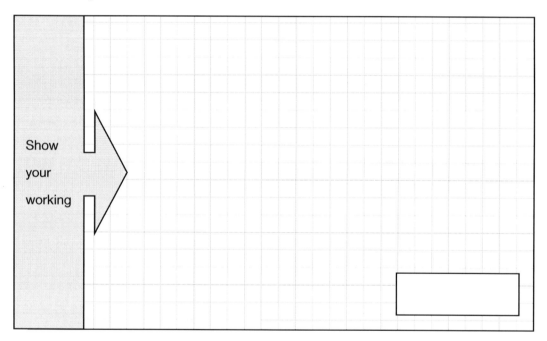

Show
your
working

QUESTION 6

Using a factor tree, express 54 as a product of its prime factors.

QUESTION 7

Place the following numbers in the correct part of the diagram.

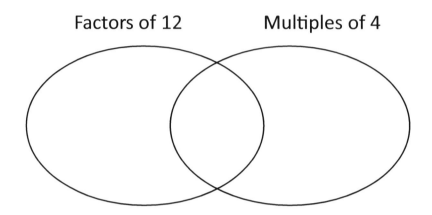

12   8   36   40   48   84   6   2

Factors of 12   Multiples of 4

QUESTION 8

Find the **lowest common multiple** for the following pairs of numbers.

a)

7 and 9

b)

12 and 8

c)

6 and 21

QUESTION 9

What is the **lowest common multiple** of 7, 14 and 21?

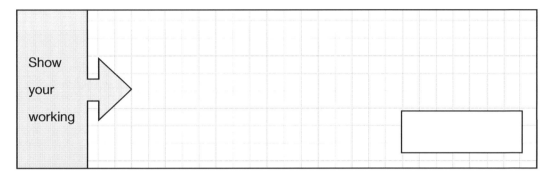

QUESTION 10

I think of a prime number between 10 and 20. I double it. Rounded to the nearest ten, the number is 20. What number did I start with?

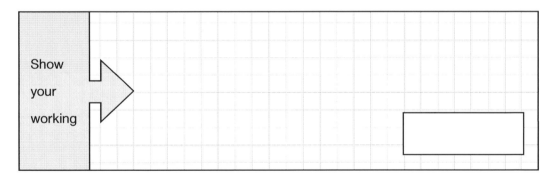

QUESTION 11

Write the first 10 multiples for the following numbers:

a) 7

b) 12

c) 15

Answers

Q1.

17 and 5

(These are the only numbers that can only be divided by 1 and itself).

Q2.

45   5   18   30   15

(These numbers are all factors of 90).

Q3.

24

*First few multiples of 8 = 8, 16, **24**, 32, 40…*

*First few multiples of 12 = 12, **24**, 36…*

So the lowest common multiple of 8 and 12 is 24.

Q4.

- 163 = YES
- 57 = NO
- 149 = YES

Q5.

24

Factors of 72	Factors of 48
• 1 x 72	• 1 x 48
• 2 x 36	• 2 x **24**
• 3 x **24**	• 3 x 16
• 4 x 18	• 4 x 12
• 6 x 12	• 6 x 8
• 8 x 9	

Q6.

2 x 3 x 3 x 3

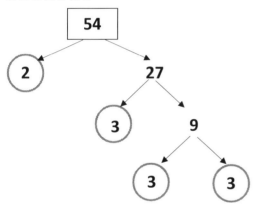

Q7.

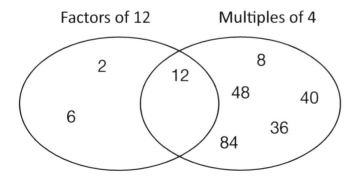

Q8.

a) 63

b) 24

c) 42

Q9.

42

*Multiples of 7 = 7, 14, 21, 28, 35, **42**, 49, 56, 63, 70, 77, 84, 91*

*Multiples of 14 = 14, 28, **42**, 56, 70, 84, 98*

*Multiples of 21 = 21, **42**, 63, 84*

Q10.

11

(You think of a number (11). You double it (22). Rounded to the nearest 10 is 20.)

Q11.

a) 7, 14, 21, 28, 35, 42, 49, 56, 63, 70

b) 12, ,24, 36, 48, 60, 72, 84, 96, 108, 120

c) 15, 30, 45, 60, 75, 90, 105, 120, 135, 150

HOW ARE YOU GETTING ON?

THE
REVISION
SERIES

SQUARED AND CUBED NUMBERS

SQUARED NUMBERS

Square numbers are numbers that are multiplied by themselves!

Squared numbers are usually represented by this symbol: ^{2}.

This is known as the 'POWER OF'.

For more information on powers, please check out the next chapter!

2 x 2 = 4   *3 x 3 = 9*   *5 x 5 = 25*

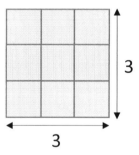

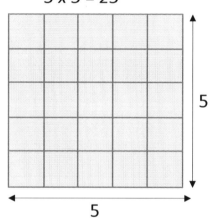

- $1^2 = 1 \times 1 = 1$
- $2^2 = 2 \times 2 = 4$
- $3^2 = 3 \times 3 = 9$
- $4^2 = 4 \times 4 = 16$

- $5^2 = 5 \times 5 = 25$
- $6^2 = 6 \times 6 = 36$
- $7^2 = 7 \times 7 = 49$
- $8^2 = 8 \times 8 = 64$

The number you have after doing the multiplication is called the **SQUARED NUMBER.**

SQUARE ROOTS

The square root of a number is a number that can be multiplied by itself, in order to give a square number.

1 2 9 16 25 36 49 64 81 100

Above is a list of the first few **SQUARED NUMBERS**.

HOW TO WORK OUT THE SQUARE ROOT:

Let's take the squared number 49.

To work out the square root of that number, you are basically trying to find what number was multiplied by itself in order to reach that number.

The square root of 49 is 7.

SQUARE ROOT SYMBOL

$$\sqrt{} \qquad \sqrt{25}$$

The square root of 25 is 5. (5 x 5 = 25)

CUBED NUMBERS

A cubed number is a number that is multiplied by itself THREE times! This is great for working out the VOLUME of 3D shapes!

Cubed numbers are usually represented by this symbol: ^{3}.

This is known as the 'POWER OF'.

For more information on powers, please check out the next chapter!

1 x 1 x 1 = 1   *2 x 2 x 2 = 8*   *3 x 3 x 3 = 27*

    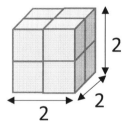   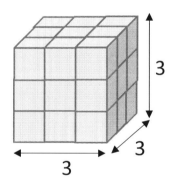

- $1^3 = 1 \times 1 \times 1 = 1$
- $2^3 = 2 \times 2 \times 2 = 8$
- $3^3 = 3 \times 3 \times 3 = 27$
- $4^3 = 4 \times 4 \times 4 = 64$
- $5^3 = 5 \times 5 \times 5 = 125$
- $6^3 = 6 \times 6 \times 6 = 216$
- $7^3 = 7 \times 7 \times 7 = 343$
- $8^3 = 8 \times 8 \times 8 = 512$

The number you have after doing the multiplication is called the **CUBED NUMBER**. The **CUBE ROOT** is the number that is multiplied to give you the cubed number.

Question Time!

QUESTION 1

Complete the table below by filling in the missing numbers. <u>The first one has been done for you.</u>

X	x^2	x^3
5	25	125
_____	49	_____
_____	_____	512
11	_____	_____
_____	144	_____

QUESTION 2

Work out the answers to the following questions.

a) 6^2 _____   b) 5^3 _____

c) 9^2 _____   d) 4^3 _____

QUESTION 3

Complete the following sums.

a) $4^2 + 6^2 =$ _____

b) $7^2 + 9^2 =$ _____

c) $12^2 - 5^2 =$ _____

d) $11^2 - 8^2 =$ _____

QUESTION 4

For the following questions, draw a representation of the following:

a) 3^2

b) 4^4

Answers

Q1.

X	x^2	x^3
5	25	125
7	49	343
8	64	512
11	121	1331
12	144	1728

Q2.

a) 36

b) 125

c) 81

d) 64

Q3.

a) 52

- *4 x 4 = 16   6 x 6 = 36   16 + 36 = 52*

b) 130

- *7 x 7 = 49   9 x 9 = 81   49 + 81 = 130*

c) 119

- *12 x 12 = 144   5 x 5 = 25   144 – 25 = 119*

d) 57

- *11 x 11 = 121   8 x 8 = 64   121 – 64 = 57*

Q4.

a) $3^2 =$

b) $4^4 =$

THE REVISION SERIES

THE POWER
OF POWERS

POWERS

Powers are a great way to write things in SHORTHAND.

We have just used a few examples of powers in the previous chapter!

Powers are simply numbers which are multiplied by themselves however many times it says.

- $10^1 = 10$.
- $10^2 = 10 \times 10 = 100$
- $10^3 = 10 \times 10 \times 10 = 1,000$
- $10^4 = 10 \times 10 \times 10 \times 10 = 10,000$

- '10 to the power of 1'
- '10 to the power of 2'
- '10 to the power of 3'
- '10 to the power of 4'

Key things to remember:

- A number to the power of 0 is always 1. ($3,853^0 = 1$)
- A number to the power of 1 is just the number itself. ($635^1 = 635$)
- The number 1 to any power will still be 1. ($1^{312} = 1$)
- If you have a negative power, turn the number upside down, and make the negative power a positive. ($6^{-4} = \dfrac{1}{6^4} = \dfrac{1}{1296}$)

ACTIVITY TIME!

Work out the number based on the following powers:

- $393^0 =$ _____
- $54,240^1 =$ _____

THE POWER OF POWERS 117

THE RULES OF POWERS

MULTIPLICATION

If you are multiplying two numbers which contain powers, you will ADD them.

EXAMPLES

$5^2 \times 5^4 = 5^{2+4} = 5^6$

$3^5 \times 3^{-4} = 3^{5+(-4)} = 3^1$

In the second example, because we are dealing with a negative power, we will just minus.

DIVISION

If you are dividing two numbers which contain powers, you will SUBTRACT them.

EXAMPLES

$5^4 \div 5^2 = 5^{4-2} = 5^2$

$3^5 \div 3^{-4} = 3^{5-(-4)} = 3^9$

In the second example, because we are subtracting a negative number, we must remember that two minus signs change to a + sign, so therefore we will add.

NOTE: These rules can only be applied if the numbers (not the powers) are the same.

IF ONE POWER IS RAISED TO ANOTHER

If one power is raised to another, you must MULTIPLY them.

EXAMPLES

$(4^3)^2 = 4^{3\times2} = 4^6$

$(4^5)^{-2} = 4^{5\times(-2)} = 4^{-10}$

In the second example, we are dealing with a raised negative number. Therefore when you multiply the numbers, the answer will be a negative raised number.

Question Time!

QUESTION 1

Simplify the following calculations:

a) 5^2 x 5^7

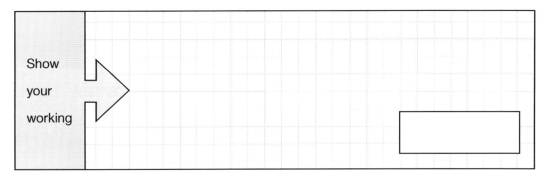

b) 9^8 x 9^{-3}

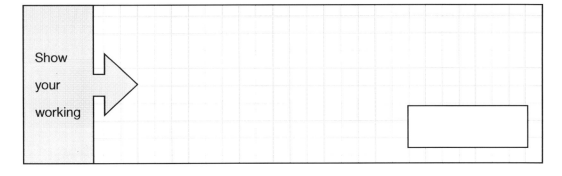

c) $6^{13} \div 6^7$

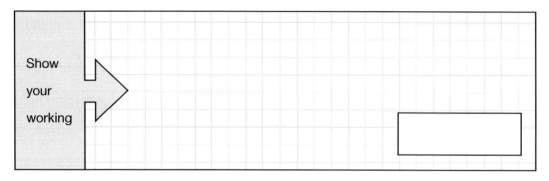

d) $(x^8)^{-6}$

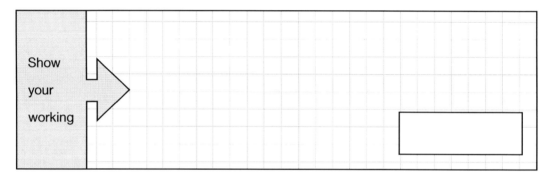

QUESTION 2

Work out the following calculations:

a) $9^3 + 6^4$

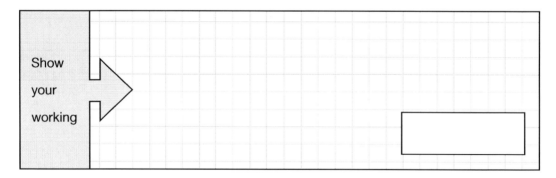

b) $3^5 - 5^2$

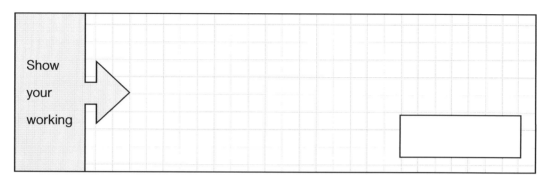

Show your working

c) $2^4 + 4^3$

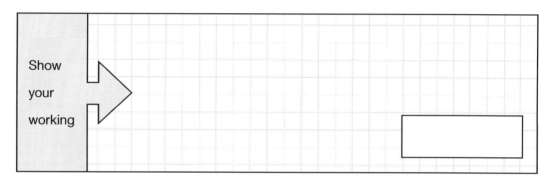

Show your working

d) $5^4 - 6^3$

Show your working

QUESTION 3

Simplify the following calculations:

a) $8^6 \times 8^{10}$

b) $(x^6)^4$

c) $9^{11} \div 9^7$

d) $(8^4 \times 8^{12}) \div 8^2$

QUESTION 4

Circle whether the statement is **true** or **false**.

a) A number to the power of 1 is ALWAYS 1.   **TRUE / FALSE**

b) When you multiply, you will ADD the powers.   **TRUE / FALSE**

c) The power of 10 means adding that many zeros.   **TRUE / FALSE**

d) If you raise one power to another, you divide.   **TRUE / FALSE**

Answers

Q1.

a) 5^9

- When you multiply, you will need to ADD the powers. (5^9)

b) 9^5

- When you multiply which contains a negative power, you will subtract the powers.

c) 6^6

- When you divide, you will subtract the powers.

d) x^{-48}

- You will need to multiply the two powers, and because one of the powers is negative, the power in your answer will be negative.

Q2.

a) 2,025

- 9 x 9 x 9 = 729
- 6 x 6 x 6 x 6 = 1,296
- 729 + 1,296 = 2,025

b) 218

- 3 x 3 x 3 x 3 x 3 = 243
- 5 x 5 = 25
- 243 − 25 = 218

c) 80

- 2 x 2 x 2 x 2 = 16
- 4 x 4 x 4 = 64
- 16 + 64 = 80

d) 409

- 5 x 5 x 5 x 5 = 625
- 6 x 6 x 6 = 216
- 625 − 216 = 409

Q3.

a) 8^{16}

- When you multiply, you will need to ADD the powers.

b) x^{24}

- When you are raising one power to another, you will need to MULTIPLY the two powers.

c) 9^4

- When you divide, you will need to SUBTRACT the two powers.

d) 8^{14}

- $(8^{16}) \div 8^2 = 8^{14}$

Q4.

a) A number to the power of 1 is ALWAYS 1.   **FALSE**

b) When you multiply, you will ADD the powers.   **TRUE**

c) The power of 10 means adding that many zeros.   **TRUE**

d) If you raise one power to another, you divide.   **FALSE**

HOW ARE YOU GETTING ON?

THE
REVISION
SERIES

FRACTIONS, DECIMALS AND PERCENTAGES

FRACTIONS, DECIMALS AND PERCENTAGES

Fractions, decimals and percentages are all ways of describing PART of a whole number.

You can convert between fractions, decimals and percentages, and you need to learn how to do this!

FRACTION	DECIMAL	PERCENTAGE
$1/2$	0.5	50%
$1/4$	0.25	25%
$3/4$	0.75	75%
$1/3$	0.3333…	$33\,1/3\%$
$2/3$	0.6666…	$66\,2/3\%$
$1/5$	0.2	20%
$2/5$	0.4	40%
$1/10$	0.1	10%
$2/10$	0.2	20%

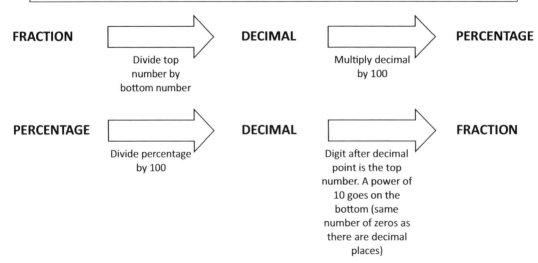

FRACTION → DECIMAL
Divide top number by bottom number

DECIMAL → PERCENTAGE
Multiply decimal by 100

PERCENTAGE → DECIMAL
Divide percentage by 100

DECIMAL → FRACTION
Digit after decimal point is the top number. A power of 10 goes on the bottom (same number of zeros as there are decimal places)

FRACTIONS

A fraction is **PART** of a whole number.

A **FRACTION** is made up of **2** numbers.

$\frac{2}{5}$ ⟶ The top number is called the NUMERATOR.
⟶ The bottom number is called the DENOMINATOR.

THE NUMERATOR

The numerator number tells you how many 'bits' we are <u>trying to work out</u>.

THE DENOMINATOR

The denominator number tells you how many bits there are '<u>altogether</u>'.

$\frac{1}{0}$ $\quad$ $\frac{1}{2}$ $\quad$ $\frac{1}{3}$ $\quad$ $\frac{1}{4}$

$\frac{1}{2}$ $\quad$ $\frac{1}{3}$ $\quad$ $\frac{1}{4}$

$\frac{1}{3}$ $\quad$ $\frac{1}{4}$

$\frac{1}{4}$

EQUIVALENT FRACTIONS

Equivalent = 'the same as'.

Equivalent fractions look different, but are actually representing the same thing.

$\dfrac{1}{2}$

$\dfrac{2}{4}$

$\dfrac{4}{8}$

As you can see, the above fraction bars demonstrate the same amount being shaded in, but they are just written in a different way. Obviously $\frac{1}{2}$ is easier to understand than $\frac{4}{8}$, but they do mean the same!

You can make equivalent fractions by multiplying or dividing the top AND bottom number, by the SAME number.

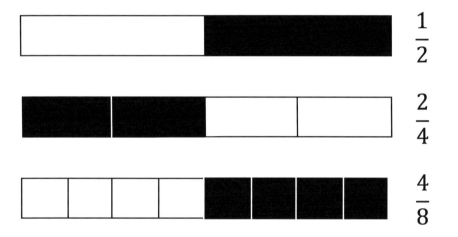

$$\underset{\times 5}{\overset{\times 5}{\frac{3}{4}}} = \underset{\times 4}{\overset{\times 4}{\frac{15}{20}}} = \frac{60}{80} \qquad \underset{\times 3}{\overset{\times 3}{\frac{1}{5}}} = \underset{\times 9}{\overset{\times 9}{\frac{3}{15}}} = \frac{27}{135}$$

SIMPLIFYING FRACTIONS

The word **SIMPLIFYING** simply means 'to make it simple'. Sometimes, you can simplify fractions in order to make them easier to understand.

This is similar to finding equivalent fractions. However, instead of multiplying, you will divide – you want to make the fraction smaller!

To simplify fractions, you will need to divide the top AND bottom number, by the SAME number.

$$\overset{\div 4}{\frac{60}{80}} \overset{}{=} \overset{\div 5}{\frac{15}{20}} = \frac{3}{4} \qquad \overset{\div 9}{\frac{27}{135}} = \overset{\div 3}{\frac{3}{15}} = \frac{1}{5}$$

$$\underset{\div 4}{\quad} \quad \underset{\div 5}{\quad} \qquad \underset{\div 9}{\quad} \quad \underset{\div 3}{\quad}$$

- To work out whether a fraction is in its simplest form, you will need to keep dividing, until no number is able to be divided into both the top and bottom number of the fraction

ORDERING FRACTIONS

In order to work out which fraction is bigger or smaller, you will need to make the bottom numbers of the fraction the same. Remember, whatever you do to the bottom number, you must do to the top.

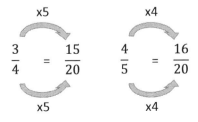

$$\overset{\times 5}{\frac{3}{4}} = \frac{15}{20} \qquad \overset{\times 4}{\frac{4}{5}} = \frac{16}{20}$$

$$\underset{\times 5}{\quad} \qquad \underset{\times 4}{\quad}$$

1) Find a number that both 4 and 5 go into = 20.
2) Because you've changed the bottom number, you need to multiply the top number by how ever many it took to reach 20.
3) So $\frac{4}{5}$ is bigger than $\frac{3}{4}$.

MIXED AND IMPROPER FRACTIONS

MIXED FRACTIONS have both an integer and a fraction.

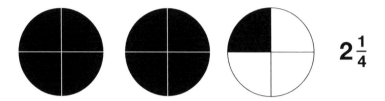

$2\frac{1}{4}$

An **IMPROPER FRACTION** is where the top number of the fraction is bigger than the bottom number of the fraction.

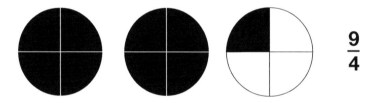

$\frac{9}{4}$

To write a mixed fraction as an improper fraction:	To write an improper fraction as a mixed fraction:
$4\frac{2}{3}$	$\frac{16}{5}$
• Multiply the whole number by the bottom number of the fraction (12). Add the top number of the fraction (12 + 2 = 14). • This number will form the top part of the fraction. • Leave the bottom number of the fraction as it is: $\frac{14}{3}$	• How many 5s go into 16 exactly? Answer = 3 • How many is left over? Answer = 1 • So, 3 is the whole number. • 1 is the top part of the fraction, and the bottom number will be the same: $3\frac{1}{5}$

ADDING AND SUBTRACTING FRACTIONS

CROSSBOW METHOD

$$\frac{3}{4} + \frac{2}{5} = \frac{15+8}{20} = \frac{23}{20} = 1\frac{3}{20}$$

Draw two diagonal lines through both of the fractions as shown. (This forms the CROSS which looks like a multiplication sign).

It tells you to multiply the 3 by 5 = 15
It tells you to multiply the 4 by 2 = 8.

Then draw your BOW (from the bottom number of the first fraction to the bottom number of the second fraction).

Again, multiply these two numbers: 4 x 5 = 20

$$\frac{4}{7} - \frac{1}{3} = \frac{12-7}{21} = \frac{5}{21}$$

Draw two diagonal lines through both of the fractions as shown. (This forms the CROSS which looks like a multiplication sign).

It tells you to multiply the 4 by 3 = 12
It tells you to multiply the 7 by 1 = 7.
12 - 7 = 5

Then draw your BOW (from the bottom number of the first fraction to the bottom number of the second fraction).

Again, multiply these two numbers: 7 x 3 = 21

MULTIPLYING AND DIVIDING FRACTIONS

ARROW METHOD

$$\frac{5}{9} \times \frac{3}{5} = \frac{15}{45} = \frac{3}{9} = \frac{1}{3}$$

Draw an arrow through the two top numbers and multiply.
5 x 3 = 15

Draw an arrow through the two bottom numbers.
9 x 5 = 45

Done! (Some fractions will be able to be simplified, as shown in the above example).

$$\frac{4}{7} \div \frac{3}{4} = \frac{4}{7} \times \frac{4}{3} = \frac{16}{21}$$

This is actually quite simple. Turn the second fraction upside down. Change the divide sum to a multiply, and then use the SAME method as if you were multiplying.

You will get the answer correct every time!

Key thing to remember:

When you are dividing two fractions, don't forget to turn the second fraction UPSIDE DOWN before you multiply the numbers.

WORK OUT A FRACTION OF A NUMBER

To find a fraction of something:

1) Divide the whole number by the bottom number of the fraction.

2) Then, multiply by the top number of the fraction.

Alternatively:

1) Multiply the whole number by the top number of the fraction.

2) Then, divide the number by the bottom number of the fraction.

EXAMPLE

Work out $\frac{5}{8}$ of £272.

STEP 1

Divide 272 by the bottom number of the fraction (8).

- $272 \div 8 = 34$

STEP 2

Multiply 34 by the top number of the fraction (5).

- $34 \times 5 = £170.$

So, $\frac{5}{8}$ of £272 is £170.

ACTIVITY TIME!

Work out the following:

$\frac{11}{20}$ of £880 $\frac{3}{4}$ of 1,428 $\frac{6}{11}$ of 990

DECIMALS

Like fractions, decimals are another way of writing a number that is not whole.

A decimal is in fact 'in-between numbers'.

6.48 ⟶ This is in between the number 6 and the number 7.

USING PLACE VALUES

In order to work out what the decimal is representing, you should use **place values**.

These include: ***units, tenths, hundredths*** and ***thousandths***.

This is covered in the chapter about ordering numbers (page 37).

ADDING AND SUBTRACTING DECIMALS

0.5 + 0.62

How to work it out:

$$
\begin{array}{r}
0.5 \\
+\,0.62 \\
\hline
1.12
\end{array}
$$

The decimal points need to be lined up!

Your answer should begin by adding the decimal point in first, and then add up the columns from left to right.

2.46 - 1.35

How to work it out:

$$
\begin{array}{r}
2.46 \\
-\ 1.35 \\
\hline
1.11
\end{array}
$$

The decimal points need to be lined up!

Your answer should begin by adding the decimal point in first, and then subtracting the columns from left to right.

MULTIPLYING AND DIVIDING DECIMALS

2.5 x 0.2

How to work it out:

• Remove the decimal points.

  25 x 2 = 50

• Now add in the decimal points. REMEMBER, you need to work out how many numbers come AFTER the decimal point in the question.

• You should notice that two numbers come after the decimal point (the .5 and the .2).

• Therefore 2 numbers need to come after the decimal point in the answer.

  25 x 2 = 50

• So the answer would be 0.50 or 0.5. It is usually written 0.5 (the 0 at the end is not necessary.

REMEMBER: division is easy if you are dividing by whole numbers. You need to move the decimal points in both numbers the same number of places.

5.39 ÷ 1.1

How to work it out:

Move the decimal point 1 space.

53.9 ÷ 11.

- Now ignore the decimal point in 53.9, do long division and then add it in at the end.

$$
\begin{array}{r}
049 \\
11\overline{)539} \\
5 \\
0 \\
\hline
53 \\
44 \\
\hline
99 \\
99 \\
\hline
0
\end{array}
$$

Put the decimal point in the answer directly above the decimal point in the question.

$$
\begin{array}{r}
04.9 \\
11\overline{)53.9}
\end{array}
$$

ANSWER = 4.9

ACTIVITY TIME!

Work out the following:

65.96 + 45.875

3.36 x 45.2

965.23 – 54.397

80.5 ÷ 0.5

PERCENTAGES

Percentages are used to work out part of a number. For example 25% of something is equivalent to $\frac{1}{4}$ or 0.25

Percent ⟶ out of 100

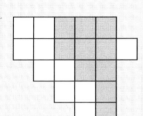

- To work out what percentage of this shape is shaded, you first need to work out the total number of squares.

Total number of squares = 20.

- Now work out the number of squares shaded.

Number of squares shaded = 10.

- There are 20 equal parts which means each square represents 5% (5 x 20 = 100). So, 5% x 10 (shaded squares) = 50%

FIND X% OF Y

To work out the percentage of a number, i.e. 35% of 300, you should ALWAYS use the following method, as it guarantees that you get the correct answer.

35% of 300

Step 1 = 300 ÷ 100 = 3

Step 2 = 3 x 35 = 105.

Step 3 = 105 is 35% of 300.

Alternatively, you can convert the percentage into a decimal. So 35% become 0.35 x 300 = 105.

EXPRESSING *X* AS A PERCENTAGE OF *Y*

To express a number as a percentage of something else, you will need to divide *x* by *y* and then multiply by 100.

Write 30p as a percentage of £1.20

Step 1

Convert the pounds into pence. You need to work with the same units.

Step 2

Divide 30p by 120p.

$30 \div 120 = 0.25$

Step 3

Multiply this by 100.

$0.25 \times 100 = 25\%$

ACTIVITY TIME!

Work out the following:

- What is 75% of £900?

- Express 98p as a percentage of £3.50.

- What is 125% of 1,200?

- What is 110% of 5,000?

- Express 12 as a percentage of 180. Write your answer to 2 d.p.

Question Time!

QUESTION 1

Patrick earns £300 in two weeks. He spends 30% of his earnings on clothes for his upcoming holiday. How much did Patrick spend?

£220	£75	£115	£90	£100

QUESTION 2

Match each box to the correct answer.

$\frac{1}{2}$ of 950		640
$\frac{2}{3}$ of 960		1,300
$\frac{3}{4}$ of 3,000		475
$\frac{5}{7}$ of 1,820		2,250

QUESTION 3

Write the following numbers in order of size, starting with the smallest.

25%   0.5   1/5   75%   0.1

QUESTION 4

Express 62 as a percentage of 2,000.

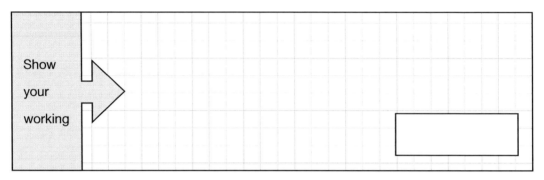

QUESTION 5

Work out which is the greater value:

$\qquad$ 60% of 2,800

Or

$\qquad$ 3/5 of 2,500

Explain your answer.

QUESTION 6

India says that $\dfrac{3}{7}$ is bigger than $\dfrac{2}{3}$.

Is she right?

Explain your answer.

QUESTION 7

Complete the table below. Write the fractions in their simplest form.

FRACTION	DECIMAL	PERCENTAGE
		1%
	0.30	
3/5		

QUESTION 8

Match the boxes from the top row to the bottom row that have the same value. <u>The first one has been done for you</u>.

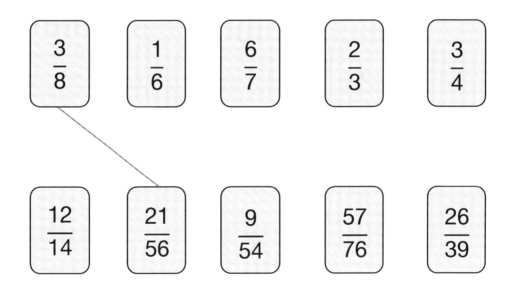

QUESTION 9

Shade in 1/4 of the shape below.

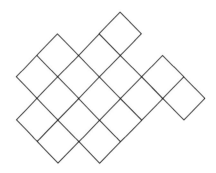

QUESTION 10

Calculate the following:

a) $2\dfrac{5}{6} + \dfrac{2}{4} =$

b) $1\dfrac{6}{7} - \dfrac{2}{3} =$

c) $\dfrac{3}{8} \times \dfrac{11}{14} =$

d) $\dfrac{3}{5} \div 6 =$

QUESTION 11

Calculate the following:

a) Express 24p as a percentage of £5.80. To 2 d.p.

b) 639.64 + 48.36

c) Find 18% of $160

Answers

Q1.

£90

- $300 \div 100 = 3$
- $3 \times 30(\%) = 90$

Q2.

1/2 of 950 = 475

2/3 of 960 = 640

3/4 of 3,000 = 2,250

5/7 of 1,820 = 1,300

Q3.

0.1   1/5   25%   0.5   75%

- 25%
- $0.5 = 50\%$
- $1/5 = 20\%$
- 75%
- $0.1 = 10\%$

Q4.

3.1%

- $62 \div 2,000 = 0.031$
- $0.031 \times 100 = 3.1\%$

Q5.

60% of 2,800 is the greater value

- 60% of 2,800 =   2,800 ÷ 100 = 28   28 x 60 = 1,680
- 3/5 of 2,500 =   2,500 ÷ 5 = 500   500 x 3 = 1,500
- So, 60% of 2,800 is the greater value.

Q6.

- You need to find a number that both 7 and 3 go into = 21.
- So 3/7 becomes 9/21
- 2/3 becomes 14/21
- So India is NOT right because 2/3 is bigger than 3/7

Q7.

FRACTION	DECIMAL	PERCENTAGE
1/100	0.01	1%
3/10	0.30	30%
3/5	0.6	60%

Q8.

3/8 = 21/56

1/6 = 9/54

6/7 = 12/14

2/3 = 26/39

3/4 = 57/76

Q9.

Shade in any 4 squares

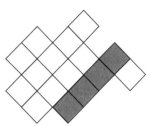

Q10.

a) $\dfrac{80}{24} = 3\dfrac{8}{24} = 3\dfrac{1}{3}$

EXPLANATION $= 2\dfrac{5}{6} + \dfrac{2}{4} = \dfrac{17}{6} + \dfrac{2}{4} = \dfrac{68+12}{24} = \dfrac{80}{24} = 3\dfrac{8}{24} = 3\dfrac{1}{3}$

b) $\dfrac{25}{21} = 1\dfrac{4}{21}$

EXPLANATION $= 1\dfrac{6}{7} - \dfrac{2}{3} = \dfrac{13}{7} - \dfrac{2}{3} = \dfrac{39-14}{21} = \dfrac{25}{21} = 1\dfrac{4}{21}$

c) $\dfrac{33}{112}$

EXPLANATION $= \dfrac{3}{8} \times \dfrac{11}{14} = \dfrac{33}{112}$

d) $\dfrac{3}{30} = \dfrac{1}{10}$

EXPLANATION $= \dfrac{3}{5} \div \dfrac{6}{1} = \dfrac{3}{5} \times \dfrac{1}{6} = \dfrac{3}{30} = \dfrac{1}{10}$

Q11.

a) 4.14%

- 24 ÷ 580 = 0.041379   x 100 = 4.1379   2 d.p. = 4.14

b) 688

c) $28.80

- 160 ÷ 100 = 1.6   1.6 x 18 = 28.8

STANDARD FORM

STANDARD FORM

Standard form is a great way to write really LARGE or really SMALL numbers.

RULES FOR USING STANDARD FORM

1) The first number ALWAYS has to be between 1 and 10.

2) The nth power (the n sign next to the 10) is based on how many places the decimal point moves.

3) The nth power is POSITIVE for big numbers, and NEGATIVE for small numbers.

$$A \times 10^n$$

Number between 1 and 10   The n symbol is the number of places the decimal point moves.

EXAMPLE 1

Express 346,000 in standard form.

STEP 1

Move the decimal point so that the first number is between 1 and 10.

- 3.46 $(1 \le A < 10)$

STEP 2

Count how many places the decimal point has moved = 5.

This gives us 10^5

STEP 3

So we have 3.46 x 10^5

EXAMPLE 2

Express 0.000346 in standard form.

STEP 1

Move the decimal point so that the first number is between 1 and 10.

- 3.46 ($1 \le A < 10$)

STEP 2

Count how many places the decimal point has moved = 4.

This gives us 10^4

Because we are dealing with a small number, the nth power will be negative = $^{-4}$

STEP 3

So we have 3.46×10^{-4}

Key things to remember:

- If you are dealing with a large number, the nth term with be POSITIVE.

- If you are dealing with a small number, the nth term with be NEGATIVE.

- If you are asked to work out a calculation which contains standard form, you will need to first work out the number, and then do the calculation.

- If you are asked to write out numbers from smallest to biggest, you will need to make sure all of the numbers are written in standard form. Next you will group the numbers with the same POWER, and order them accordingly. Lastly, arrange the groups of numbers based on the front number.

| $3.4 \quad \times \quad 10^3$ | = | 3400 |

| $5.6 \quad \times \quad 10^{-4}$ | = | 0.00056 |

Question Time!

QUESTION 1

Express 986,000 in standard form.

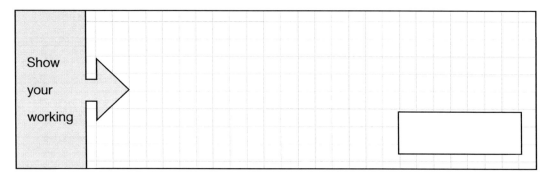

QUESTION 2

Express 0.000457 in standard form.

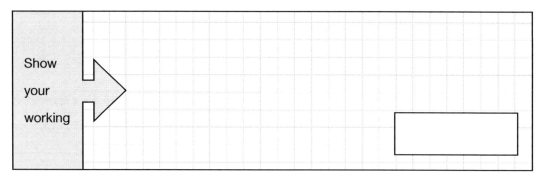

QUESTION 3

Change this number from its standard index form to its actual number.

6.24 x 10^8

QUESTION 4

Change this number from its standard index form to its actual number.

3.97×10^{-5}

QUESTION 5

Change this number from its standard index form to its actual number.

7.79×10^{-4}

QUESTION 6

Change this number from its standard index form to its actual number.

1.43×10^{3}

QUESTION 7

Arrange these numbers in order from smallest to biggest.

$$3.35 \times 10^{5} \qquad 6.34 \times 10^{-3} \qquad 5530 \qquad 0.00035$$

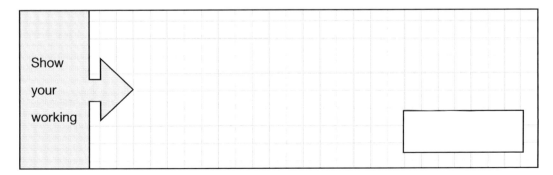

Show your working

Answers

Q1.

9.86×10^5

Q2.

4.57×10^{-4}

Q3.

624,000,000

Q4.

0.0000397

Q5.

0.000779

Q6.

1,430

Q7.

0.00035 6.34×10^{-3} 5,530 3.35×10^5

- 3.35×10^5 = 335,000
- 6.34×10^{-3} = 0.00634
- 5.53×10^3 = 5,530
- 3.5×10^{-4} = 0.00035
- So smallest to biggest = 0.00035 6.34×10^{-3} 5,530 3.35×10^5

HOW ARE YOU GETTING ON?

THE
REVISION
SERIES

CALCULATOR
BUTTONS

CALCULATOR BUTTONS

Here is a quick breakdown of some of the most useful calculator buttons you should be aware of.

Above is a SCIENTIFIC CALCULATOR. Whilst it is unlikely that you will use this advanced calculator in KS3, you will be expected to use this in GCSE, so it is great to get to know this calculator in more detail.

SHIFT BUTTON

Press this button FIRST if you want to use something written above a button.

E.g. (Shift) + (=) will give you (%)

SQUARE, CUBE AND ROOT

Work out the squared and cubed numbers by pressing a number and one of these signs.

BRACKETS

Use brackets if you are doing multiple operations (i.e. important in BIDMAS)

PI

Press (shift) and (π). This is equivalent to the number 3.141...

FRACTIONS

For a fraction, press the first number followed by this button and then the next number (to form your fraction).

You may need to press the (shift) button first.

MEMORY

(STO, RCL & M+)

If you are working out multiple calculations, and you need to remember the first answer, you can move on to the next calculation and then push this button to add, subtract etc.

NEED A LITTLE EXTRA HELP WITH KEY STAGE THREE (KS3) MATHS?

How2Become have created these other FANTASTIC guides to help you and your child prepare for their Key Stage Three (KS3) Maths assessments.

FOR MORE INFORMATION ON OUR KEY STAGE 3 (KS3) MATHS GUIDES, PLEASE CHECK OUT THE FOLLOWING:

WWW.HOW2BECOME.COM

WANT TO TAKE A LOOK AT OUR KEY STAGE (KS3) ENGLISH GUIDES?

How2Become have created these other FANTASTIC guides to help you and your child prepare for their Key Stage Three (KS3) English assessments.

FOR MORE INFORMATION ON OUR KEY STAGE 3 (KS3) ENGLISH GUIDES, PLEASE CHECK OUT THE FOLLOWING:

WWW.HOW2BECOME.COM

Get Access To
FREE
Key Stage 3
Resources

www.MyEducationalTests.co.uk

Printed in Great Britain
by Amazon